DIARY

OF A

MINECRAFT

ENDERMAN

Book 1

Endermen Rule!

by Pixel Kid and
Zack Zombie

Monday

Hi, my name is Elliot and I'm an Enderman.

You know, people don't know much about Endermen.

I think it's because we're naturally the strong, silent type.

But because we're so mysterious, people say some really crazy stuff about us.

Like, people think that Enderman play basketball because we're tall and have long arms.

But it's not true. We don't play basketball.

But if we did, we would kick your butts. Ha-Ha!

1

Another thing people say is that we steal people's stuff.

Now, just because we move your block around doesn't mean we're stealing it.

We just think that it would look better somewhere else.

I mean, it's true that sometimes we take your stuff home.

But that's only because it probably looks better in our house than yours.

I've also heard people say that we're always staring at you.

And I even heard people say that if you stare at us, we'll melt your face off.

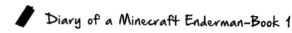

Now, that's not true. We just stare because we're just really impressed at how perfectly square your head is in Minecraft.

And about melting your face off. . .

Well, that only happens if you look at us funny.

Now, it is true that we can teleport.

But we can't teleport to the moon or anything like that.

The most we can teleport is only a few feet.

Mostly, we just use it for really important stuff.

Like farting and teleporting away before someone can blame it on us.

Tuesday

Today, I started thinking about where Endermen come from.

I tried asking my mom, but she just stared at me.

I tried to ask my other Endermen relatives, too.

But every time I asked them, they just stand there staring out into space.

Gets really annoying sometimes.

Yeah, something tells me that nobody knows where Endermen come from.

Now, a kid at school once told me that Creepers and Endermen actually came from a secret military experiment.

They tried to make us into super soldiers and something went wrong.

Like, Creepers were supposed to have explosion power.

And Endermen were supposed to have teleportation and mind control powers.

But Creepers ended up with stinky farts, and they randomly explode.

And Endermen. . .well, we just stare out into space a lot and have sticky fingers.

He gave me a picture of what Endermen looked like before the experiment.

After seeing it, it made me think that maybe he was right.

But I have my own idea of where Endermen came from.

I think Endermen were created when a magical wizard used magic ink to draw a stick figure one day.

Then, when the Wizard wasn't looking, the stick figure drew more stick figures that multiplied into a whole new civilization, and took over the world.

Don't ask me how I know this, I just do.

Some of the other kids think I'm crazy.

But when you look at a stick figure, you can see the resemblance, can't you?

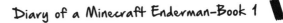

Now, I heard Notch say that Endermen are cousins of Slenderman.

But I don't believe that.

I mean, sure, you can't stare at Slenderman for too long or he'll melt your face off.

And sure, we're both tall, dark and mysterious.

And sure, we both have long arms.

And sure, we both sneak up on you when you're not looking.

And sure, we can both teleport.

And sure, our names sound real alike.

And sure. . .

Hey, wait a minute. . .

Whoa! Are you kidding me?!!

Wednesday

Today I was hanging out with my family, and I was just thinking how lucky I am.

That's because Endermen families are pretty cool.

Now, in my family there's my mom and dad, and their names are Aliyah and Nigel Enderman.

And there's my little sister, Ebony.

Except my sister is not so little.

She's taller than me.

In Endermen families, the women are a lot taller than the men.

I don't know why.

But I think it's because their feet are bigger.

Endermen families aren't very big, though.

At least not around here, anyway.

But back home in The End, we have family everywhere.

Like, I've got lots of uncles, aunts and a ton of cousins.

And when I go home on vacation, I always meet new cousins I've never met before.

It's like they just pop up out of nowhere.

So far, I've counted 57,334 cousins.

But they look so much alike, I probably counted some of them twice.

Having a lot of relatives comes in handy, though.

We have the best dance parties.

The Mosh pits are awesome!

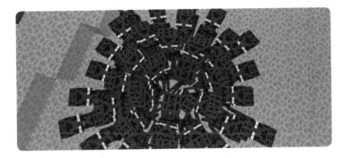

My mom and dad like to do a lot of fun stuff with our family.

Like, they wanted us to join a circus once.

They thought we would make great acrobats.

'The Flying Endermans' was what they called us.

13

We even had shirts made up.

But the circus people changed their minds after the first time we tried it.

It's really hard grabbing each other when you don't have any fingers.

Yeah, Endermen don't have fingers or hands.

We just grab blocks by balancing them on our long arms.

Makes it really hard when we have an itch, though.

So, I get mad when people say that Endermen have "sticky fingers."

Obviously, they don't know what they're talking about.

Thursday

Today, I started the first day of my new school.

I actually go to school for gifted kids.

It's because I'm, well. . . gifted.

Naw, it's just another way of saying that Endermen are different.

You see, we can't go to school with the other Villager kids.

The schools just aren't safe for us.

Like, one time they started a Student Exchange program with The End.

And there was an Enderman that wanted to check out regular Villager school.

But it didn't go so well.

Like, the first day he got there he had to be taken to the hospital.

You see, first he hit his head on the doorway on the way into the school.

And he kept hitting his head on the ceilings in every classroom.

He even got his legs all mangled trying to fit in one of the "desk chairs" they had at school.

Then, he caused an explosion in the chemistry lab when he tried to grab a beaker full of chemicals.

Yeah, when they designed Villager school, they didn't have Endermen in mind.

But the school I go to is perfect for Endermen.

The doorways are really tall.

The classroom ceilings are really tall, too.

We even have tall stools and high desks that we can't get mangled by.

And they give us Velcro gloves in chemistry class so we won't drop anymore beakers.

So cool.

But the only thing I don't like is Gym class.

Like, the only sport they let Endermen play is basketball.

I really don't know why. . .

Villager kids are welcome to come to our school, though.

But they usually don't go because they feel kind of small.

Only one Villager kid ever came to our school and graduated.

He fit right in.

But he did feel awkward sometimes, though.

Friday

Today I had to take my pets to the Mob veterinarian because they were feeling blue.

Yeah, normally they're purple, so I knew something was probably wrong.

Now I have the coolest pets in the world.

They're so cool, I carry them around with me wherever I go.

They're called Endermites, and they're really friendly.

Though, I don't think they're friendly to Minecraft players.

Once there was a bully in our neighborhood who bothered me a lot.

He kept saying that he wanted to destroy me to get an Ender pearl.

Which I thought was kinda gross.

Especially since Endermen poop Ender pearls.

I mean, he didn't have to be a bully about it.

I would've gladly given him my poop if he asked nicely.

But he started swinging his sword at me.

So I teleported to get away from him.

But then I realized I dropped my Endermites.

Next day, I found my Endermites with pieces of that kid's skin in their teeth.

That'll show him not to mess with Endermen.

. . .Or their poop.

Saturday

Today I was going to play a practical joke on my sister.

I had to get her back for putting a silverfish in my toilet.

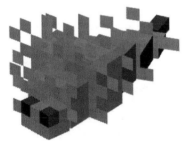

If you didn't know, Endermen really like to play practical jokes.

We play a lot of them on Minecraft players all the time.

One of my favorite games is called "Teleport Tag."

That's when we teleport next to you, smack you on the head, then teleport away.

Classic!

Another game I really like is called, "Timber."

That's when we wait for you to build the biggest, coolest Minecraft creation ever.

Then we take away the most important blocks holding it together.

The fun part is teleporting behind you and yelling, "TIMBER!"

But you know, the one game that Endermen are really bad at is a game called "Follow the Leader."

We tried it once.

But it didn't end very well.

Man, I miss those guys.

But my favorite game of all time is the "Staring Contest."

We just look at you for a while and see how long you can stare back at us without blinking.

You can make all kind of faces and noises, but whoever blinks first loses.

And I'm like the all-time Minecraft champion at this game.

Wanna play?

Okay. Get ready. . .now!

Wow, you're good!

Not bad!

Whoa! You're a natural!

Ha... made you blink!

I told you I was good at this game.

Sunday

Today I went to hang out with one of my Mob friends.

Now, not all my friends are Endermen. I have a friend named Quentin, and he's a Creeper. And he's really cool.

A little stinky sometimes, but cool.

Quentin and I sometimes talk about what would happen if you merged a Creeper and an Endermen together.

That would be so cool.

We would call him an Endercreeper, or a Crenderman. Or maybe a Creeperman?

He would have the power to teleport, read minds, and cause massive explosions with his mind.

And if he farts, he can teleport away before anyone found out it was him.

We even drew a picture of it. . .

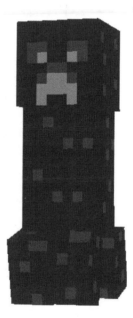

Cool, right?

Monday

Last night, the weirdest thing happened.

Like, out of nowhere, it started flashing lightning and crackling thunder outside.

The neighbors said something about all the Zombies from the neighborhood going crazy and attacking the Villagers next door.

33

Everybody was yelling about a Zombie Apocalypse.

But I think they were lying.

I saw the whole thing, and I didn't see any Zombies with lips.

My mom said that strange stuff like that happens to Mob kids when they reach puberty.

I believe her, too.

Like, recently, I started sleepwalking for no reason.

And every morning, I wake up and find all this stuff in my house.

So weird. . .

Tuesday

Today I was thinking that if I had the power to do anything, I would probably make my arms a little bit shorter.

That's because right now, my arms reach all the way down to my ankles.

It gets kind of hard to do a lot of stuff.

Like, I have a real hard time scratching my nose when it itches.

Not to mention, when I have to pee...

Sigh...so wrong.

Also, if I had the power to do anything, I would make all the doorways in the Overworld really tall.

I've hit my head so many times walking into people's houses, my head is black and blue.

Can you see what I mean?

What do you mean, what's the big deal?

My head is normally pink, you know.

The other thing I would do is get rid of my fear of water.

Yeah, it's true, Endermen are afraid of water.

I try not to tell anybody because it's so embarrassing.

But sometimes I can't hide it.

Like, one time, we went on a school field trip at the lake.

When all the kids went swimming, I made an excuse that I was allergic to swim trunks.

But I think the other kids found out because the next day at school they brought their squirt guns.

One of the guys took a picture of what I looked like that day. . .

Like I said. . .embarrassing.

Nobody really knows why Endermen are afraid of water.

My dad said that Endermen don't like water because a long time ago, when the first Endermen migrated to the Overworld, he went to the lake and was attacked by a squid.

Ever since then, Endermen tell their children that giant monster squid are just waiting to

drag them to the bottom of the lake if they go swimming.

Yeah, Endermen families are little dysfunctional.

Personally, I don't like water because I don't like taking baths.

And the giant monster squid thing is pretty scary, too.

But I guess if I wasn't so afraid of water I would probably smell better.

But I don't sweat it.

Teleporting comes in really handy for those smelly moments.

Wednesday

In just a few more days, it's going to be Halloween.

And Halloween is like my favorite holiday.

The best part about Halloween is that I can dress up like cool characters.

This year, guess who I'm going as?

Yeah, I couldn't help myself. I had to be Slenderman for at least one Halloween.

Me and my friends sometimes like to play a game called 'Hide and Sneak' during Halloween.

I'm really good at it, so I always win.

All the other kids keep saying it's not fair because of my teleportation skills.

But what can I say? I'm gifted.

But recently, for some reason, my friends started wearing pumpkins on their heads when we play.

43

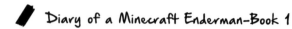

Now it's like totally impossible to find those guys.

I don't know. . .maybe I'm losing my touch.

Thursday

Today, one of my friends at school asked me what my favorite food is.

Now my favorite food in the whole wide world is licorice.

And my favorite kind of licorice is black licorice.

I don't know why, but it's sooooooo good.

I think somebody out there was thinking of me when they made black licorice.

My other favorite food is cookies.

I know, I know, I have a sweet tooth.

What can I say?. . .I'm only eleven years old.

My grandma makes the best cookies, though. I think she puts love in every one.

And a ton of sugar, yeah!

But I really like her cookies because she makes them look like me.

Cool, right?

The cool thing is that Endermen don't eat vegetables, meat, or stuff like that.

We can live on licorice and cookies for a long time.

Only problem is the sugar does a number on our teeth, though.

See what I mean?

Friday

Today we're going to go visit my grandparents in The End.

My mom and dad even said I could leave school early today.

I'm glad, too.

I'm starting to get really sick of basketball.

Now I grew up in The End, and it was a lot of fun.

The best part is that my village was right next to where the Ender Dragon lived.

Now, we didn't see the Ender Dragon most of the time. It normally just kept to itself.

But once a month it had to do its duty.

And like most birds, it did it in midair, right over our village.

Now, the Ender Dragon didn't poop Ender pearls or even gunpowder.

Our Ender Dragon pooped black licorice, yeah!

And the best kind of licorice is raw, warm Ender nuggets.

Yum! Those are the best!

Now, we moved to the Overworld when I was a little kid.

My dad got a job in construction, and my mom got a job as a teacher at the School for Gifted Mobs.

Yeah, I know, that's my school.

And it is kind of weird seeing my mom at school every day.

But she makes up for it by bringing me warm Ender nuggets to snack on.

Yum!

But when I grow up I want to be in construction like my dad.

Something about moving blocks around makes me feel like I was meant for it.

Now, my grandpa and grandma Enderman have a candy shop in The End.

It's the biggest candy shop in the whole city.

When I normally come to visit, I eat as much black licorice as I can get my hands on.

But they don't mind, though.

The Ender Dragon is really busy making a lot of deposits this year.

Saturday

Today I had a sleep over at my friend Quentin's house.

Quentin's family is really cool.

Actually, his dad is a famous inventor.

I think he invented the first Creeper energy drink.

Though, I think after they started selling it, they realized that Creeper energy drinks were not a very good idea.

When I got to Quentin's house, we decided to play a game of throw and catch in his backyard.

Unfortunately, the game lasted for about three seconds.

But I really like sleepovers at Quentin's house, though.

The only problem is that I don't get a lot of sleep most of the time.

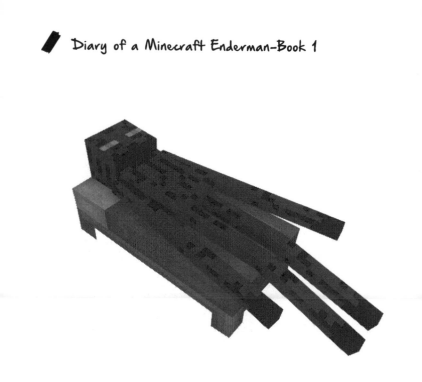

Sunday

Today I was thinking about my all-time favorite hero in the whole wide world. . .

. . .Jack Skellington.

Yeah, Jack is so cool.

I mean, I don't know what it is but there's just something about him that I can really relate to.

It's like he gets me, you know?

My other favorite hero is guy named Chuck Norris.

He's mad cool.

My dad watches his movies all the time.

And he can do some real cool stuff with his hands and feet.

Like I said. . .awesome.

Monday

Today, the teacher made us write a paragraph about "If you could change one thing in Minecraft, what would it be?"

Now, if I could change one thing in Minecraft, I would probably make everybody taller.

It's really hard being the tallest Mob around.

You always hear people say the same things whenever you walk into a room.

Things like:

"Wow. . .you're tall."

"How's the weather up there?"

"Do you play basketball?"

"Can you reach that for me?"

"Where do you buy your clothes?"

"How tall are you. . .really?"

"You must hit your head, a lot."

"You have a booger in your nose."

And when you trip, somebody somewhere always yells, "Timber!!!"

Now being taller than everybody else does have its perks.

Like, I always get the best apples from the top of the tree.

And when I'm tired, I can rest my elbows on people's square heads.

Still it would be nice to have people in Minecraft be my size.

At least people would stop getting mad at me for looking down on them all the time.

The nerve. . .

Tuesday

I was on the computer today, and I couldn't believe all the lies that people say about Endermen.

Some of the stuff people are saying out there are just not true.

And, honestly, some of it is just insulting.

Like, here are a few of the rumors I've heard on the internet. . .

WANNA DO STARING CONTEST?

LOOK AWAY AND YOU DIE

You don't die when you look away during a staring contest with an Enderman.

But if you lose and don't pay, well, that's another story.

You see, there's another person saying that we took his stuff.

We don't take people's stuff!

We just move it around to a nicer spot.

Yeah, sometimes it ends up in our house, but that's because it looks better at our house than yours.

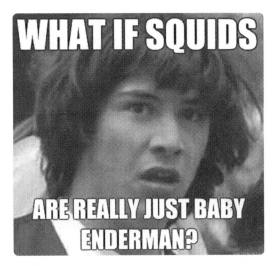

Now see, that's just wrong.

Endermen don't look anything like those creepy black things with long tentacles. . .

65

I think your hairstylist is an alien.

The nerve. . .

Wednesday

Today, I, uh. . .had a little bit of an accident.

Like, you know how I told you that Endermen like to play practical jokes?

Well, I really didn't think anybody would mind. . .

I mean, how did I know the giant spider would escape?

And how did I know it would kidnap my entire 7th grade class?

And how did I know that it was really hungry because it was feeding time at the zoo?

Well, it happened like this. . .

Today was our school field trip to the Minecraft Hostile Mob Zoo.

And the biggest hostile Mob they had on a display was a giant spider named Kong.

And Kong was special because he was a genetically modified mutant spider.

I heard he was a mix between a cave spider, a silverfish, an endermite, and a guardian.

That's right, that means even if you fall in the water, Kong will still eat you.

Yeah, my worst nightmare.

And I know what you're thinking. . .

And the answer is no; if Kong bites you, you won't turn into Spiderman.

I know. A zombie friend of mine tried.

He's had a really hard time in school ever since.

He said something about it being really hard getting used to walking around with eight legs.

Anyway, a few of the kids in my class were daring each other to see who could get really close to Kong's cage.

It was all just fun and games until Sam opened his big mouth.

Sam really gets on my nerves.

If you didn't know, Sam is a Shulker. And I grew up with him in the End.

And, yeah, he's my nemesis.

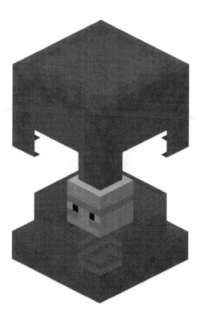

"I bet Elliot can't do it," Sam said. "He's too chicken."

"Oh yeah?"

"Yeah!"

"Well watch me," I said.

This is so easy, I thought. *I could just teleport to the cage, touch it, and come back. That'll show him who's boss.*

But then, as I was getting ready, Sam said the words that I knew would mean my total and utter destruction.

"Oh, and you can't use your powers."

"Huh?"

"See, I told you he was a chicken," Sam said. "Ha, ha, ha!"

Then all the other kids started laughing at me, too.

"Oh yeah, well, watch me," I said, not really know what was coming out of my mouth.

"Oooooooh!" all the kids yelled out.

Now, you're probably wondering where all the adults were when all this was going on.

Yeah, I'm still wondering that.

So then, I had a decision to make. Was I going to do the 'Walk of Doom' to the spider cage or the 'Walk of Shame' back to school?

So, I started slowly walking to the spider cage.

"Look! Elliot's doing it!" the kids yelled.

And with every step I took, I could see the spider licking its lips.

I probably looked like one big, fat piece of licorice to him.

At least my long arms give me an edge, I thought. *I could just stay far enough away and then use my long arms to touch the cage.*

That is until. . .

"You can't use your arms either," Sam said.
"You've got to touch it with your head like
the rest of us."

Oh, brother, I'm dead.

Wednesday, Later That Day. . .

Well, my luck turned around.

As I was slowly getting closer and closer to the cage, one of my Endermites dropped out of my pocket.

I tried not to step on it and I accidentally tripped, falling head-first toward the cage.

"BOP!"

"Yeaaaaaahhh!" all the kids yelled as my head hit the cage.

It hurt like crazy, but I proved to Sam and the other kids that Endermen rule!

Now it was my turn to bring the pain. . .

"Your turn, Sam. Oh, what's the matter, Sammy? You aren't chicken, are you?"

"Do it! Do it! Do it!" all the kids started yelling.

I guess the pressure finally got to Sam, so he started walking toward the cage.

Except this time, I thought a little practical joke would help scare him real good.

"Do it! Do it! Do it!"

So while all the kids were chanting, and Sam was walking to his utter death, I teleported behind the cage and removed some of the bars.

I can't wait till Sam gets real close, I thought. *That spider's tentacle is going make him jump out of his shell, ha, ha!*

At least, it seemed like a good idea at the time. . .

Wednesday, Even Later That Day. . .

BANG!

BUNG!

CRANK!

CRUNG!

BOOM!

Well, you probably guessed it. . .

Kong broke out of his cage.

I think it was because the bars I removed. . . uh. . .were holding up the whole cage.

Oops.

"AAAAAAAH!!!!!"

"Everybody run!"

Fisk! Fisk! Fisk!

"AAAAAAAH!!!!!"

Fisk! Fisk! Fisk!

Everybody at the zoo went crazy.

Uh. . .remember I told you that it was feeding time at the Zoo?

Well, it was a few minutes before Kong's feeding time when he got out.

So I think our 7th grade mob class must've looked like a giant bag of Skittles to him. Because next thing I know, Kong just started picking them off one by one like a kid in a candy store.

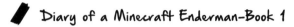

Then he wrapped the kids up in his purple spider webs and put them on his back like a fanny pack.

I was kind of far away, so I thought I was safe. But for some reason I couldn't move.

Then I looked down, and I was stuck in a spider web!

Talk about a living nightmare.

Kong looked at me with his eight eyes.
And then he started crawling closer in my
direction.

I was sure I was going end up as his afternoon
snack. I mean, who doesn't like a nice long
stick of black licorice?

So I closed my eyes and awaited my fate.

But after a few seconds, I opened my eyes
and Kong was gone.

I guess he didn't like black licorice. . .

Weirdo.

Thursday

They cancelled class today because of what happened at the zoo.

So I went to go visit Quentin, and I told him everything that happened.

"Man, I wanted to get back at Sam," I said. "But not like this."

"What are you going to do now, Elliot?" Quentin asked me.

As we were talking, the TV was on in the background. Then I heard a newsflash come on the TV.

"Breaking news! Kong, the giant mutant spider, was spotted in the mountains of the Forest Biome. Scientist believe that Kong is

trying to return to her original home where she was captured, to hatch her eggs."

"Whoa! Kong is a girl?!!!!!"

"Scientist believe that the children, which she captured from a Mob school field trip, are safe until she finds her resting place and uses the captured children as food for her newborn babies. Unfortunately, the Forest Biome Troopers are finding it difficult to maneuver through the rough mountain terrain, which is delaying the rescue of the children. More news at 11."

"Well, at least it sounds like the kids in your class are safe," Quentin said.

"But not for long. As soon as Kong gets home, its dinnertime."

"Do you think the troopers are going to get to them in time?" Quentin asked me, looking worried.

"I don't know. But maybe I can."

"Dude! You can't teleport that far," Quentin said. "And even if you do, you're like only 11 years old. How are you going to battle a ginormous genetically modified mutant spider?"

"I have to do something; it's all my fault."

"But, Eliot, can you even teleport that far?"

"I don't know. The farthest I've ever teleported was to the principal's office and that was for a game of Teleport Tag."

"Yeah, that was funny. The principal never knew what hit her," Quentin said. "Sigh. . .good times."

"But you know, one time I had a dream that I teleported to the moon," I said.

"So what happened?"

"Well, when I woke up my feet smelled like cheese."

Quentin just gave me a weird look.

I think it was because my feet always smell like cheese.

But then Quentin remembered, "Dude! I just remembered! My dad's been working on a potion in his garage that can boost a Mob's powers. He also said it will grow some serious hair on your chest. He called it the Ender-Boost."

So then me and Quentin snuck into his dad's garage.

"Whoa!"

The garage was awesome. There were all kind of brewing stands with potions brewing.

Then we both looked up at this dark-purple-colored potion with a big X on the front.

"There it is!" Quentin said, grabbing the potion.

"Are you sure this is safe?" I asked him.

"Well, it'll either work or you'll grow some serious hair on your chest. So either way, you win."

Then he handed me the potion.

Well. . .here goes nothing.

Gulp!

So, I drank it all down. It wasn't bad. Kinda tasted like an Enderberry smoothie with a lemon twist.

"Well, we need to test it to see if it works," Quentin said. "Do you know where you're going to teleport?"

"Yeah, they said that Kong was in the mountains, in the Forest Biome."

"Well, let's give it a test," Quentin said, putting on a suit of armor and hiding behind some boxes.

Great. Talk about inspiring confidence.

Anyway, I clenched my butt cheeks really tight and concentrated really hard on where I wanted to go.

Then suddenly. . .

BAMF!

Thursday, Later That Day. . .

I guessed I concentrated too hard. . .

Next thing I knew, I was in my grandma's house, in the End.

I think it was because I started thinking about how some Ender nuggets would taste really good right now.

Also, I think that Ender-Boost potion did something to me.

No, it didn't grow hair on my chest.

It grew hair on my hands. . .

That's what I said. . .HANDS!

I turned into an Ender-mutant!

It was so weird.

Kinda felt like I had sausages on my arms.

87

Man, so much for trying to help my friends, I thought.

Not only was I really far away from where the kids were, but now I'm a weirdo and I can't help anybody.

So, I just sat on my hands and cried.

If I ever get out of this, I promise to never play a practical joke ever again, I thought.

I was just hoping that somebody out in Mojang would hear me and come to my rescue, just this once.

But who was I kidding?

It was hopeless.

All of sudden, a small shiny purple cloud appeared out of nowhere.

Then it grew bigger and bigger until it filled the whole room.

What in the world is happening? I thought.

The next thing I know, some guy jumped out of the purple cloud.

Then I heard action music playing.

"Who are you?" I asked the man dressed in a commando outfit.

"Well, I'm known by many names but you can call me Chuck Norris."

"What the what?!!! The real Chuck Norris?"

WHEN THE BOOGEY MAN GOES TO BED AT NIGHT...

HE CHECKS UNDER THE BED FOR CHUCK NORRIS

"Yep, in the flesh. And I'm here to help you, son."

"I don't know what to do," I said in between sobs. "I got my friends in trouble, and now I don't know how to help them."

"Sounds like a real predicament you got yourself into," Chuck said.

"What am I supposed to do?"

"Well, like I always say, 'If you ever get your friends in trouble, you deserve a roundhouse kick to the face.'"

"Wait. . .what?"

"Or like my daddy always used to say," Chuck continued, "'There's no problem too big that you can't punch your way out of. . .and if you don't, you deserve a roundhouse kick to the face.'"

"Huh?"

"Or like my grandmamma used to always say, 'Eat your greens or I'll roundhouse kick you in the face.'"

Then Chuck looked right at me with a really intense stare.

I don't know how, but I had a strong feeling what was coming next.

So before I got roundhouse kicked in the face, I clenched my butt cheeks real tight and teleported my way out of there.

BAMF!

Next thing I know, I was outside of a giant cave in the mountains, in the Forest Biome.

I couldn't believe it. I made it!

Thank you, Chuck Norris. . .wherever you are.

Friday

It was Friday, and I could tell I was in the right cave because of all the purple spider webs everywhere.

As I walked closer, I could hear the spider noise getting louder and louder.

Fisk, Fisk, Fisk.

Fisk, Fisk, Fisk.

Fisk, Fisk, Fisk.

As I slowly crept into the cave, I eventually made it to a big cavern.

And there was Kong, on top of a hill, sleeping.

Fisk, Fisk, Fisk.

Fisk, Fisk, Fisk.

Fisk, Fisk, Fisk.

I walked around her enormous body to see if I could find the other kids, but I couldn't find them anywhere.

BOP!

Suddenly, out of nowhere, a Zombie arm hit me on the head.

Fisk, Fisk, Fisk!

Kong woke up briefly to see what the commotion was about. But, luckily, she went back to sleep.

When I looked up to see where the arm came from, I couldn't believe it. All the kids from my class were in a giant purple spider web that was hanging from the ceiling.

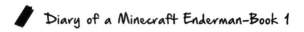

I was trying to wave at them to get their attention, but they all looked asleep.

The bigger problem was that hanging right next them there was a ginormous purple egg sack with like a million spider eggs.

. . .And it was throbbing.

Gross.

The eggs looked all fat and gooey, like if they were about to open up any minute.

So I had to do something fast.

BAMF!

I teleported up to the spider web holding the kids, but it started creaking.

CREEAAAKKK.

Fisk, fisk, fisk!

Kong woke up because of the noise, but eventually she went back to sleep again.

Phew! Okay, I'm up here, but how am I going to get the kids out? I thought.

Then I remembered Chuck Norris' words. . .

"There's no problem too big that you can't punch your way out of. . .and if you don't, you deserve a roundhouse kick to the face."

Oh, man, I've never punched anything before in my life; now, how am I supposed to punch a web?

Well, here goes nothing. . .

So, I bunched up my new sausage fingers and punched the spider web.

It worked! I made a hole in it.

Then I stuck my fingers in the web and started pulling it apart.

Whoa! Hands are so cool!

But, I think I pulled on the web too hard.

Next thing I know, one of the skeleton kids slipped out and was hanging by one of his ribs.

And, it didn't help when he woke up. . .

"AAAAAAHHH!!!!!"

Then all the other kids woke up. . .

"AAAAAAAHHHHH!!!!"

And then Kong woke up. . .

Fisk! Fisk! Fisk!

Then all the kids started screaming and shaking the web, and it started creaking and swinging.

Next thing we know, we swung over and slammed right into the big egg sack.

SPLOOSH!

Some of the eggs burst open and we all got covered in purple goo.

Blech.

Then all of a sudden, the baby spiders started coming out of their eggs!

There was like a million of them crawling out.

And every time we swung over, they tried to grab us.

"AAAAAAAHHHHH!!!!"

So now we had a million baby spiders trying to eat us.

And we had Kong on the bottom of the cavern waiting for us.

Not only that, the purple goo made it really hard to hang on. . .

Then, I slipped. . .

Aaaaaaaahhhhhhh!

Flump!

Luckily, I landed on a large pile of bones on the cavern floor.

But then as I started getting up, a giant shadow surrounded me.

I really didn't want to turn around. . .but I knew I had to.

And right when I did turn around, Kong's face was right in front of me!

Fisk, Fisk, Fisk!

So there she was, staring at me with those eight giant black mysterious eyes.

But even though everything inside of me was telling me to teleport away…

I decided, it was time for the ultimate staring contest.

It was time to stare death in the face!

So now, it was on like Donkey Kong.

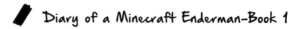

After about ten minutes, me and Kong just kept on staring at each other.

I could hear all of the kids yelling in the background.

They were yelling something about how the baby spiders were forming a spider bridge to reach them.

But I couldn't be distracted because I was in the staring battle of a lifetime.

Suddenly. . .

Blink, blink, blink, blink, blink, blink, blink, blink.

Kong blinked!

I won!

Yeah, I know it didn't mean much because I was going to die. But, at least I would die knowing that Endermen rule!

Then all of a sudden. . .

Fisk, fisk, fisk, tee hee.

Wait. . .what was that?

Fisk, fisk, fisk, tee hee hee . . .

I couldn't believe it, but I think Kong was laughing!

Then Kong came up really close to me and put her head down in front of me.

It's a good thing I had those man-hands. So, I used my sausage fingers to scratch her head.

Next thing I know, she flipped over and so I scratched her belly too.

Fisk, fisk, fisk, tee hee hee.

"HELP US!"

Oh, man, the other kids!

I looked up and the baby spiders had already reached my friends. I was too late!

Then, the baby spiders started to grab the kids one by one.

I had to close my eyes, so I wouldn't see the horror!

But, suddenly, instead of eating them. . .

. . .The baby spiders just started bringing the kids down safely to the ground!

Huh?!!

Finally, when the last of the kids were down, the baby spiders started singing and laughing. Then they just jumped on their backs like they wanted their bellies scratched.

So then me and the other kids just spent the rest of the time laughing, singing, and scratching spider bellies.

But then, out of nowhere, some huge lights shined around us.

"ALL RIGHT, MEN, TAKE YOUR POSITIONS!"

Oh no! It was the Forest Biome Troopers!

Kong ran to a corner, and all her babies ran under her for protection.

Then all the troopers took their positions and got ready to take Kong and her babies down.

I could hear them racking their guns and preparing to fire.

Chuck-Chack!

Me and the other kids were all really scared. We all knew that Kong and her babies were in trouble, but we couldn't do anything about it.

So, I looked over at Sam the Shulker, and he looked back and gave me a nod. Then we

looked at the other kids, and they all gave a nod.

Then me, Sam, and all the other kids jumped in front of Kong and her babies to protect them. We all locked arms not knowing what would happen to us.

Then we closed our eyes, and hoped for the best...

Suddenly, the Trooper in charge started yelling.

STAND DOWN!

STAND DOWN!

Then all the troopers put their guns down.

Kong and all her babies were so happy, they started jumping, laughing, and singing. They were singing and laughing so loud that you could hear it throughout the cave.

Then Forest Biome Troopers were so moved, that they joined in and started laughing and singing too.

So we all spent the entire night laughing, singing, and scratching spider bellies.

It was awesome!

And man. . .it sure beat getting roundhouse kicked in the face.

Saturday

Well, all the kids finally got home safe and sound.

The good thing was that nobody got hurt.

Except for the Zombie kid that lost his arm.

We found out later it was just a rental, so it was all good.

They decided not to bring Kong back to the Zoo.

She had too much responsibility taking care of all her new babies.

So they just set up an animal hospital up in the mountains so they could help her.

Also, they changed her name because Kong sounded too scary.

Now they just call her Princess, which is still kinda creepy but cool.

The Forest Biome Troopers were so moved by Kong and her babies that they passed a law protecting all spiders in the Forest Biome.

The Forest Biome troopers also got a surprise when some of Kong's babies volunteered to be Troopers.

So now, instead of Zombie horses, the Forest Biome Troopers ride spiders.

Cool, right?

And after that whole situation, Sam and me started hanging out more.

We realized that we had a lot more in common than we thought.

So now, instead of my nemesis, Sam's like one of my best friends.

I think what really made the difference was when he finally realized that Endermen Rule!

Yeah!

Well, my hands are back to normal, too.

It seems like the Ender-Boost wore off.

And I'm really glad, too.

Having fingers is really dangerous.

I mean, there are just too many things around to stick your finger into.

But I really miss playing one of my new favorite games.

It starts by asking somebody to pull your finger. . .

I also found out that one of the side effects of the Ender Boost was hallucinations.

So, I'm not sure if Chuck Norris was real or not.

But it doesn't really matter. . .he's always going to be my hero.

But the one thing I did learn from this crazy situation is that I need to be a little more careful when I play practical jokes on people.

I mean, like they can really backfire.

And now that I think of it, I should probably stop trolling people's houses. . .

And I should probably stop playing Teleport Tag. . .

And I should probably stop moving people's stuff. . .

And I should probably. . .

Naaaaaa.

It's just way too much fun!

Epilogue

So hopefully after reading this, you have a better understanding of what it's like to be an Enderman.

And all those rumors you've heard about us? Yeah, well, they're not true.

I mean, sure, we stare. . .but we do it to let you know how much we admire your perfectly square head.

And sure, we teleport. . . but that's only because we don't want to get blamed for cutting the cheese.

And sure, we move your stuff. . .but its only because it'll look better somewhere else. . .like our house.

But Endermen are kind and playful souls that would love to play with you one day.

So, how about a staring contest?

Ha. . .made you blink!

THE END.

Find out What
Happens Next in...

Diary of a Minecraft Enderman
Book 2

Coming soon...

If you really liked this book, please tell a friend. I'm sure they will be happy you told them about it.

Leave Us a Review Too

Please support us by leaving a review. The more reviews we get the more books we will write!

Check Out Our Other Books from Pixel Kid Publishing:

Diary of a Minecraft Creeper Series

Get the Entire Series on Amazon Today!

96802545R00069

Made in the USA
San Bernardino, CA
21 November 2018